NOT FROM HERE

International Students' Cookbook

Not From Here Cookbook
Department of Information Studies
University College London
Gower Street
London, WC1E 6BT

First published in Great Britain by Not From Here Cookbook in 2016

A catalogue record for this book is available from the British Library.

Paperback ISBN 978-0-905937-20-5

Printed and bound by SLS Print

Notfromherecookbook.tumblr.com
@NFHCookbook

NOT FROM HERE
International Students' Cookbook

UCL Students

SLS Print: London

CONTENTS

AFRICA   67

ASIA   73

LETTER FROM THE EDITORS

Hungry? Homesick? Here's the solution.

Food has a memory. Food binds people together. It is a deeply personal thing, and so much more than just cooking for sustenance. We all have memories of special gatherings with family and friends, and more often than not, those memories are associated with food.

The food we make on a daily basis is an extension of ourselves, our families, and our culture. In times of celebration, crisis, or even when we just need a bit of comfort, food can play a major role in our lives. When we are far from home, food can bring us back.

We wanted to source the recipes that mean the world to people, the recipes that bring them back home, and curate them into one cookbook. We also wanted to share the memories merged with the recipes because they are just as important as the food itself.

The inspiration behind this cookbook came from a desire to bring international students together and to help people feel at home at a time when they are far away from loved ones.

Browsing through the bookshops, we noticed something was missing from the shelves. There were cookbooks which instructed students on what to make, endorsed here and there by chefs, but we couldn't find a cookbook that offered personal recipes from students. We wanted to fix this. This is what sets us apart from the other cookbooks out there. This is an international students' cookbook, published by students, with students, and for students.

Every recipe in this book is special to someone and they have generously shared this with you, dear reader! We want to say a

massive thank you to our contributors who have kindly shared their delicious recipes and meaningful memories with the world.
The NFHCookbook team have personally made each and every single recipe in this book from scratch. We've had a lot of fun baking, melting, rolling, chopping, bubbling, mashing, roasting, stewing, braising, kneading, stirring, steaming, poaching, peeling, whisking, frying, glazing, and cooking and we hope you will too!

Thank you for purchasing Not From Here: The International Students' Cookbook. We hope that you'll enjoy experimenting with the recipes, whether you're making something special for friends or just trying out something new.

All the best,
The NFH Cookbook Team

ACKNOWLEDGEMENTS

The completion of this book would not have been possible without the help and support of so many wonderful people.
Our heartfelt thanks goes out to Dr Daniel Boswell, for putting our group together and helping us whenever we needed it.
Dr Samantha Rayner and Dr Melanie Ramdarshan Bold, for their continuing support of our project.
Maria Vassilopoulos, for her advice and connections.
Kerstin Michaels and Ian Evans, for their administrative support.
SLS Print, for printing our book.
Everyone who submitted a recipe, without you, this book would not be nearly as delicious and diverse.
All the contributors to our Indiegogo campaign, for helping fully fund this venture.
EdAid, for promoting our project.
You, for reading the book!
Thank you so much!!!

NORTH AMERICA

One Pot Spaghetti Bolognese

Canada
by Isabel Tinkler

PREPARATION TIME
10 minutes
COOKING TIME
30 minutes

1 Dice the garlic and onion, and fry in the oil until soft. Add mince and cook until brown.

2 Add tin tomatoes, tomato puree, balsamic vinegar and basil and simmer with the lid on for 20 minutes or longer if you can to infuse all the flavours.

3 Cook the spaghetti as directed on the packet. Top the spaghetti with the bolognese and parmesan cheese. Enjoy!

Serves 4

1 tbsp olive oil
1 onion
1 garlic clove
500g mince
1 tin of whole tomatoes
1 tbsp tomato puree
1 tbsp balsamic vinegar
2 tbsp fresh basil
4 portions of spaghetti
parmesan cheese

A classic comfort food, this is a recipe that instantly reminds me of my family and home in Canada. It's not a Canadian recipe, but it's definitely my family's favourite, so it is my ultimate taste of home.

Memory by Isabel Tinkler, UCL

Nana Wight's Pumpkin Bread

Maine, USA
by Sydney Butler

PREPARATION TIME
10 minutes
COOKING TIME
60 minutes

1 Pre-heat oven to Gas Mark 4/180°C/350°F. Whisk the eggs and add the oil, water, and pumpkin and mix well. In a separate bowl, sift the flour and add the sugar, bicarbonate of soda, salt, and spices.

2 Make a well in the centre of the dry ingredients and add the pumpkin mixture. Stir well until completely mixed. Pour the mixture into greased loaf pans and bake for one hour, or until an inserted skewer comes out clean.

3 Remove the pans from the oven and set out on wire racks so the bread cools in the tins.

Makes 3 loaves

4 eggs
150ml water
165ml vegetable oil
1 can pumpkin
500g flour
2 tsp bicarbonate of
    soda
1 1/2 tsp salt
1 tsp ground cinnamon
1 tsp ground nutmeg
pinch of ground cloves
225g granulated sugar

I remember sitting rewriting this recipe card on a regular basis when I was growing up. The recipe belongs to my great-grandmother, and my mum wears it out with use during winter months. Although I never met my great-grandmother, we still use a number of her recipes and they're all absolutely delicious. They also make gigantic portions - unsurprising given that she was cooking for eighteen children.

Memory by Sydney Butler, UCL

Orange Chutney Chicken Casserole

Washington, USA
by Stephanie King

PREPARATION TIME
10 minutes
COOKING TIME
60 minutes

1 Pre-heat oven at Gas Mark 4/180°C/350°F. Prepare rice as per instructions, and cook chicken if necessary.

2 Mix in a blender the orange juice, corn flour, chutney, brown sugar, curry powder, and salt.

3 Combine cooked chicken, cooked rice, and blended sauce. Place in 9x13 cooking dish and bake uncovered for 1 hour.

Serves 8

900g cooked chicken meat,
    cut into chunks
1kg brown rice
475ml orange juice
2 tbsp corn flour
225g mango chutney
3 tbsp brown sugar
1 tsp curry powder or more
    to taste
¼ tsp salt

Sitting down to dinner together as a family was always a priority in our house, but sometimes we were all too busy to cook an entire meal from scratch every night. So when we had a hectic week coming up, my mom would make this casserole (or maybe two!) ahead of time and put it in the freezer. Then, when we all got home from our busy days, we could pop this in the microwave and still sit down to a hearty and delicious dinner together. This dish will always remind me of my family even when we're 5,000 miles apart.

Memory by Stephanie King, UCL

SOUTH AMERICA

Moqueca Stew

Brazil
by Kaysen Harlow

PREPARATION TIME
20 minutes
COOKING TIME
20 minutes

Serves 4

250g small prawns
1kg skinless white fish,
    cut into 5cm cubes
80ml lime juice
3 garlic cloves, diced
55ml olive oil
1 onion, roughly
    chopped
2 bell peppers, thinly
    sliced
2 tsp chilli flakes
2 tsp paprika
salt and pepper to taste
3 tomatoes, deseeded
    and chopped
400ml coconut milk
1 bunch of coriander,
    chopped (set some
    aside for garnish)
rice to serve

1 Place the prawns and fish in a bowl with 2 tbsp lime juice and diced garlic so that the pieces are well coated. Season with salt and pepper. Chill in the fridge for at least 10 minutes while you cook the rice.

2 In a large saucepan, heat the olive oil over a medium heat and cook the onion for two minutes. Add the bell peppers, chilli flakes, paprika, tomatoes, salt and pepper and cook until the peppers have softened. Stir in the chopped coriander.

3 Take the seafood, garlic and lime juice mixture and place it in the saucepan. Pour coconut milk over the fish and vegetables. Bring soup to a boil, reduce the heat and cover to simmer for 15 minutes. Add the remaining 2 tbsp of lime juice, taste and adjust seasonings. Garnish with coriander and serve with rice.

Some have chowder, others have bouillabaisse, but for Brazilians, we have moqueca (mo-keh-ka)! A personal favourite that reminds me of family sailing trips off the northern coast of Brazil, moqueca is a Brazilian classic that slightly differs from family to family. Made with fresh fish caught from our sailing trips, moqueca has always been at the centre of family gatherings alongside laughter, new additions, and stories

Memory by Kaysen Harlow, Cass Business School

Pan Amasado
Homemade Bread

Chile
by Rodolfo Romero

PREPARATION TIME
45 minutes
COOKING TIME
20 minutes

1 Mix the flour, yeast, and salt in a bowl and make a volcano shape, with a hole in the middle to pour the liquid into. Slightly melt the lard in the microwave until it is manageable with your hands.

2 Pour the lard, water, and milk into the bowl with the rest of the ingredients and knead until it forms a dough. At this stage, you have the option to add some seeds or herbs if you wish.

3 Cover the bowl with cling film so that no air can get through, and leave it to rest for 30 minutes. Pre-heat the oven to Gas Mark 2/150°C/300°F and line a baking tray with aluminium foil.

4 Knead the dough again, and mold into bun shapes in whatever size you want. Flatten the dough and pierce the surface with a fork.

5 Cook the dough for 20 minutes, or until the bread is golden brown. Cut a bun in half, spread some caramel on each and enjoy!

Serves 10

500g plain flour
10g yeast
1 tsp salt
100g lard
200ml warm water
caramel (manjar/dulce
    de leche)

Where my wife and I live in Chile it is very rainy. So, it is quite difficult to go out and buy bread every day, so I make it at home. Whether it is to enjoy with loved ones, or because it is pouring outside, this homemade bread is the perfect excuse to sit around a table with a cup of coffee. It is simple to prepare, and every time I make it here in London I can smell the green meadows of Dalcahue, and a little piece of home comes back to me. It is a piece of Chile in the South of England.

Memory by Rodolfo Romero, UCL

Beef and Potato Hotpot

Chile
by Macarena Herrera

PREPARATION TIME
10 minutes
COOKING TIME
50 minutes

Serves 3

4 medium potatoes
1 carrot
3 garlic cloves
1 large onion
½ pepper
4 medium tomatoes
300g diced beef
150g peas
½ tsp oregano
¾ tsp salt
1 tbsp oil
1 laurel leaf
200ml white wine (optional)
250g passata

1 Chop the potatoes, carrot, garlic, onions, pepper, and tomatoes into strips.

2 Set a large pot to a medium heat and pour in the oil. Then, add the diced beef and stir until it is completely sealed. Add the sliced carrot, onions, tomatoes, pepper, peas, garlic, oregano, laurel leaf, and the salt, and stir for a few minutes. Add the potatoes and white wine/water to the pan.

3 Put the lid on, and leave to simmer for 30 minutes. Then pour in the passata and stir. Bring the pan to a boil and then simmer. If the mixture is dry, add a cup of water. Serve in a bowl and enjoy!

The winter in Santiago, Chile, can be quite cold and dry. Some of my best memories after a long day consist of getting home and smelling this delicious hotpot made by my mother, my grandma, and later on, my mother-In-Law. All three of them spoilt me with this dish, which is comforting, filling, and tasty. I remember sitting with these three amazing women and listening to their stories, sitting at the table, sharing this hotpot and some laughter. So, now that I am studying in London, I make it every now and then to feel warm inside.

Memory by Macarena Herrera, UCL

Corviche de Atun
Tuna Fish Corviche

Ecuador
by Natalia Encalada

PREPARATION TIME
20 minutes
COOKING TIME
20 minutes

Serves 8

1 tsp oil
1 garlic clove
1 red onion
1/2 green pepper
1 tomato
1 can of tuna chunks
3 twigs of fresh coriander
cumin, black pepper and
    salt to taste
3 plantains
250g ground peanuts

1 Dice the garlic, onion, green pepper, and tomato and add to a heated, oiled pan. Season with salt and pepper and fry until softened.

2 Season the tuna fish with coriander, cumin, and black pepper to your taste.

3 Grate half of the plantains, and add the other half to boil in water until you can easily poke them with a fork. Mash the boiled plantains and mix together with the grated ones. Add ground peanuts to make a dough, and knead. Add half a glass of warm water if necessary to form the paste.

4 Take a portion of dough (about the size of the palm of your hand) and add the tuna and vegetable mix to the centre, molding the dough around it into an egg shape.

5 Deep fry the dough balls in oil, or bake the corviches in the oven at Gas Mark 4/180°C/350°F for 15 minutes or until golden.

This is a traditional Ecuadorean dish from the Manabi province. It has two main ingredients: plantain and tuna fish. Corviches could be served with your favorite salad and/or sauce. In Ecuador it is common to have them with a cup of coffee.

EUROPE

Steak Pie and Cheddar Mash

Scotland
by Kirsty Mackay

PREPARATION TIME
30 minutes
COOKING TIME
1 hour 30 minutes

Serves 4-6

PIE
800g steak, diced
6 rashers back bacon,
    sliced (optional)
2 tbsp flour
3 large white onions,
    finely sliced
400g button mushrooms,
    roughly chopped
3 large carrots, peeled
    and sliced into discs
500ml beef stock
red wine or ale
    (whatever is left over
    from the previous
    night's festivities)
375g ready to roll puff
    pastry
garlic
salt and pepper
egg, beaten with a little
    water to form an egg
    wash
olive oil

To make the pie:

1 Pre-heat the oven to Gas Mark 7/220°C/425°F. In a large pan, heat a small amount of oil and add the diced steak to sear along with the bacon if using. Dust the flour over the meat. When the meat has browned, add the onions, garlic, carrots and mushrooms. When the onions turn golden, add the stock along with a generous slug of red wine or ale. This will add flavour to the gravy. Bring to the boil, then lower the heat, allowing the mixture to simmer for 45 minutes-1 hour.

2 Meanwhile, lightly grease a casserole dish with butter. Roll out your puff pastry to the desired length. Take your pan off the heat and add contents to the deep dish. Wait a moment for the steam to settle before layering the puff pastry on top. You don't want it to break due to the heat! With a fork, poke a few holes in the pastry.

3 Using a brush or your finger, lightly glaze the top of the puff pastry with the egg wash and place in the oven

for 30 minutes until golden on top.

To make the mash:

1 Chop the potatoes in half and place in a large pan of boiling water for 35 minutes. Grate the cheddar and set aside.

2 Drain the potatoes, and add a splash of milk and butter to the pan. Mash the ingredients together until creamy and there are no lumps left. Mix in the cheddar and a small amount of mustard. Et voila. Serve the pie with the mash and enjoy!

MASH
750g potatoes, peeled
cheddar, grated
milk
dijon mustard
butter

My family would always make steak pie on New Year's Day. It's a tradition kept by many other Scottish families the day after Hogmanay. We'd rise late around 2pm (after wandering home around 6am after the bells and falling into bed). I'd cut the carrots, onions, and button mushrooms while my parents would prepare the rest for the party ahead. My parents always hosted the New Year's Day party, and their friends and children would congregate at our house around 8pm to continue the celebrations. We'd eat the pie as a family before the next bout of celebrations began. I learnt how to make steak pie by watching them. Nowadays, even if I am not home for Hogmanay, I always make it. My French husband loves it so much, we've kept the tradition.

Memory by Kirsty Mackay, UCL

Chilli and Guacamole

England
by Antonia Carr

PREPARATION TIME
20 minutes
COOKING TIME
3-4 hours

CHILLI
1 tbsp vegetable oil
2 brown onions
3 garlic cloves
500g lean beef mince
3 bell peppers (any
    colour)
1 chilli (red or green)
1 tsp ground cumin
1 tsp ground coriander
1 beef stock cube
2 tins chopped tomatoes
1 tbsp worcestershire
    sauce
salt and pepper (to taste)
2 tins kidney beans

GUACAMOLE
1 avocado
½ red onion
½ chilli (red or green)
coarse salt and pepper
    (to taste)

1 Dice onions and garlic, and fry with oil in a deep casserole pan until sweated. Add the beef mince and fry until browned. Finely dice the chilli, chop bell peppers into chunks, and add to pan to cook until softened. Add cumin, coriander and stock cube powder and cook for 1 minute.

2 Add chopped tomatoes, Worcestershire sauce and water, making sure ingredients are well mixed, and season with salt and pepper to your own taste. Bring to the boil and then simmer for 3-4 hours with the lid on, stirring occasionally and adding 100ml of water if it starts to get dry. Drain and add kidney beans 10 minutes before serving.

To prepare guacamole:

1 Remove skin and stone from avocado, and crush flesh in a small bowl with a fork. Finely dice red onion and chilli, and mix well. Add coarse salt and pepper into avocado mix to your own tasting.

SERVE CHILLI AND GUACAMOLE IN TORTILLAS WITH SALAD, OR WITH LONG GRAIN RICE AND SOUR CREAM.

I've spent many years trying to develop a decent chilli recipe, but this one is my favourite and is the first ever dish my boyfriend made for me when we started dating. It lasts for days, and is quite a life saver as a student; you can just let it cook away while you get on with assignments. It's definitely a crowd pleaser and a regular item on our menu each month!

Memory by Antonia Carr, UCL

Apple and Blackberry Crumble

England
by Zoe Sharples

PREPARATION TIME
15 minutes
COOKING TIME
55 minutes

1 Pre-heat oven to Gas Mark 5/190°C/375°F.

2 Rub flour, butter and salt together until they form a breadcrumb consistency. Then add 50g of sugar.

3 Simmer the apples with remaining sugar and a tiny bit of water until the apples start to collapse. Then add blackberries, lemon juice, and zest. Taste the fruit to check it has enough sugar.

4 Transfer fruit to an ovenproof dish and place crumble on top. Cook for 40 minutes and serve with double cream.

Serves 4

175g plain flour
110g butter
pinch of salt
75g caster sugar
3 cooking apples,
    peeled and chopped
handful of blackberries
1 lemon, juice and zest
double cream to serve

My mum used to make this recipe all the
time when we were growing up. The best
bit is always where the fruit meets the
crumble and it goes delicious and gooey.
You can try it with rhubarb if you're not a
fan of stewed apples. The lemon zest is
mightily important, so don't skip that bit!

Memory by Zoe Sharples, UCL

Welsh Cakes

Wales
by Catriona Beamish

PREPARATION TIME
10 minutes
COOKING TIME
15 minutes

1 Crumble flour, sugar and margarine/ butter together. Mix in the currants and bind with the beaten egg.

2 Roll onto a floured surface and cut into circles. Cook on a very lightly greased griddle or heavy based frying pan over a low heat. Each side is done when light brown. Dust with sugar and serve hot or cold.

Serves 6

200g flour
100g sugar
100g margarine or butter
100g currants
1 large egg

I was camping with my family one time and my mum had made a big batch of these for all of us. She left them outside the tent in a cake tin and in the middle of the night my mum and dad heard what they assume to be bears rustling around the campsite, so obviously they're terrified and tried not to make any sudden movements and hoped that they wouldn't die. When we woke up in the morning we discovered that raccoons had gotten into the cake tin and eaten all of the welsh cakes. So there you go, if they're good enough for the raccoons, they're good enough for you.

Memory by Catriona Beamish, UCL

Tomates à la Provençale
Tomatoes in the Provence fashion

France
by Pauline Cuchet

PREPARATION TIME
5 minutes
COOKING TIME
45 minutes

1 Pre-heat the oven to Gas Mark 7/ 220°C/427°F.

2 Slice the tomatoes in half and place each open-faced up on a baking tray or dish. Sprinkle each half tomato with olive oil and a layer of bread crumbs. The olive oil should help the crumbs stick to the tomato. Sprinkle each tomato with the crushed garlic and the Italian herbs.

3 Place in the oven and bake for 45 minutes, until the tomatoes have softened and the breadcrumbs are golden.

Serves 4

6 average-sized tomatoes
olive oil
bread crumbs
2 garlic cloves, crushed
mixed italian herbs

This is one of my favourite meals of all time. My mom would always make it for my birthday. I always thought she never made enough because I could have eaten the entire thing by myself. For me this recipe reminds me of having my family together.

Memory by Pauline Cuchet, UCL

La Tarte aux Pommes de Papi et Mamie
Grandma and Grandpa's Apple Tart

France
by Pauline Cuchet

PREPARATION TIME
10 minutes
COOKING TIME
25 minutes

1 Pre-heat the oven to Gasmark 7/ 220°C/425°F.

2 Line a tart tin with pastry, including the sides, and use a fork to pierce the bottom at regular intervals. Spread the apple sauce over the bottom part of the pastry.

3 Peel and slice the apples and place them in a circular pattern. Sprinkle with brown sugar and cinnamon.

4 Cook for 25 minutes, until the pastry is golden.

Serves 4-6

1 pack ready-to-roll short-
    crust pastry
4 large or 6 medium-sized
    apples
2 tbsp apple sauce
brown sugar
cinnamon

My grandma used to make this recipe for my siblings and I every Wednesday when we would visit. When she passed away, my grandpa came to live with us and would bake the tart almost every day. He would get very offended if we did not finish it, therefore, apple tart was a part of my daily diet for ten years. Now that he is gone too, I try to maintain the tradition and baking this tart always brings back fond memories of spending time with my grandparents.

Memory by Pauline Cuchet, UCL

Tarte à la Tomate
Tomato Tart

France
by Pauline Cuchet

PREPARATION TIME
15 minutes
COOKING TIME
25 minutes

1 Pre-heat the oven to Gas Mark 7/ 220°C/425°F.

2 Cover a tart tin with the pastry, including the sides, and use a fork to pierce the pastry at regular intervals. Spread the mustard over the bottom part of the pastry and sprinkle rice over the mustard. This will retain the water let out by the tomatoes while cooking.

3 Cut the tomatoes into small quarters and arrange them in a circular pattern. Slice the mozzarella and place the slices at regular intervals over the tomatoes. Sprinkle with crushed garlic and herbs. You can sprinkle a tablespoon of olive oil over the finished tart if desired.

Serves 4-6

1 pack ready-to-roll
    short-crust pastry
4 large or 6 medium-sized
    tomatoes
1 tbsp mustard
1 tbsp rice
200g mozzarella
1 garlic clove, crushed
mixed italian herbs
olive oil (optional)

4 Place tart in the oven and bake for 25 minutes, until the pastry is golden and the mozzarella is melted.

YOU CAN ADD 6 TBSP OF COUSCOUS
INSTEAD OF 1 TBSP OF RICE.
IF THERE IS A LOT OF WATER LEFT
AFTER BAKING, JUST CAREFULLY TILT
THE TIN OVER A SINK AND DRAIN AS
MUCH LIQUID AS YOU CAN.
EAT HOT OR COLD.

This is one of the first recipes
my mom ever taught me and
through the years, I have added
my own twists to it. Whenever I
feel homesick, this is my go-to
recipe as it brings back all the
flavours of home.

Memory by Pauline Cuchet, UCL

Luxembourgish Kniddelen
Dumplings

Luxembourg
by Marina Hartung

PREPARATION TIME
20 minutes
COOKING TIME
10 minutes

1 Pour the milk into a bowl and add two eggs, a pinch of salt, and pepper. Use a sieve to slowly integrate the flour into the mix, and blend it all until you have a firm dough.

2 Put water to boil in a pot and drop tablespoons of dough into the water. Once the dumplings emerge on the surface after 1-2 minutes, take them out, put them into a bowl and keep them warm in the oven/microwave to Gas Mark 1/140°C/275°F.

3 Fry the bacon in a pan, add the cream and pour over the dumplings (optional). The sweet alternative to bacon and cream is to add apple puree at the end.

Serves 4-6

500ml milk
2 eggs
600g flour
1 pinch of salt and pepper
bacon cut into little pieces
    (optional)
single cream (optional)

Loosst lech et schmaachen, as we say in Luxembourgish!

Having been born to German and Italian parents but brought up in Luxembourg, I have always lived in between those three cultures. With few Luxembourgish restaurants around (we are not particularly known for food, or known at all for that matter) I was only presented with the opportunity to try this traditional dish a few months ago after years of hearing about it. I have clearly been missing out! So, despite not being a family recipe this dish has quickly become something I crave whenever I miss the safe haven that Luxembourg has always been for me.

Zuppa Inglese
The Italian Trifle

Italy
by Filippo Bernardini

PREPARATION TIME
15 minutes
COOKING TIME
45 minutes

Serves 8

CAKE
5 eggs
150g caster sugar
80g flour
80g corn flour
pinch of salt

CREAM
4 egg yolks
130g sugar
500ml milk
vanilla pod
30g corn flour

SYRUP
50ml alchermes
20ml water

cocoa powder to decorate

1 Pre-heat your oven to Gas Mark 4/180°C/350°F. Whisk together the sugar, eggs, and salt until fluffy. Add the flour and corn flour and mix until combined. Pour the batter into a 24cm cake tin and bake for 30 minutes.

2 Meanwhile, prepare the cream by whisking the yolks with the sugar, and then add the corn flour. Pour the milk into a saucepan and add the vanilla pod. Bring the milk to the boil then turn off and let it cool for a couple of minutes before adding the egg-sugar mixture, stirring quickly until fully combined. Then pour the cream into the pan and return to the heat. Bring it to boil while stirring until it becomes solid. Take cream off the heat and let it cool completely.

3 To construct the Zuppa Inglese, cut the cake in half and put the bottom layer in a Pyrex dish (the same size as the cake). Using a tablespoon, wet the cake with the Alchermes and pour half the cream on the cake in an even layer. Repeat the layers until the dish is full or all cake and cream has been used.

4 Sprinkle the cake with cocoa powder, and your Zuppa Inglese is ready.

ALCHERMES IS A LIQUEUR WHICH IS QUITE DIFFICULT TO FIND OUTSIDE OF ITALY. YOU CAN SUBSTITUTE THIS WITH A SPICED CHERRY SYRUP, MADE FROM BOILING TOGETHER A PUNNET OF FRESH DE-STONED CHERRY HALVES, 500ML CHERRY JUICE, 250G CASTER SUGAR, 2 CINNAMON STICKS, 2 TSP GROUND CLOVES AND 1 TSP NUTMEG. LEAVE TO SIMMER FOR 1-2 HOURS UNTIL THICKENED.

Zuppa Inglese is a typical Italian dessert that can be easily found in Italian restaurants, especially in the centre of Italy. There are so many theories about its origins and many of them are connected to the English trifle. Legend has it that in the sixteenth century, an Italian diplomat returned from Britain to Ferrera, Italy, and demanded a trifle-like cake. According to another source, the zuppa inglese was created by an Italian maid working for a British family who was stationed in Florence. Whatever the truth is, the Zuppa Inglese embodies the culinary marriage of two cultures, English and Italian, and its taste makes it one of the most irresistible desserts.

Gnocchi alla Sorrentina

Italy,
by Federica Merati, Michela Pea, and Filippo Bernardini

PREPARATION TIME
40 minutes
COOKING TIME
10 minutes

1 Boil potatoes in a large pan with just enough water to cover them for 20 minutes or until tender (test with a fork). Remove potatoes, peel them while they are still hot then rice them with a potato ricer. Let the mashed potatoes cool down.

2 Place the mashed potatoes on a wooden board, add flour, egg, and a pinch of salt. Use your hands to combine the ingredients, forming into a dough. Let the dough stand for 15 minutes and then cut into 8-10 pieces. Roll each piece with your fingers to create an evenly distributed rope. Chop the ropes into small pieces, about twice the size of a marble. Press the fork prongs on top of the pieces to create ridges.

Serves 6

1kg potatoes
300g flour
1 egg
pinch of salt
tomato sauce
basil
mozzarella

3 Place the finished gnocchi into a large pot of salted boiling water and cook until they float to the top (approximately 2-4 minutes). Remove the gnocchi to a separate dish. In the meantime, prepare classic tomato sauce with basil and chop the mozzarella into small bites. When the gnocchi are ready, mix in the sauce and sprinkle mozzarella on top.

Rumor has it that gnocchi were first invented by Alessandro Volta. The famous scientist brought potatoes from America and grew them in his fields in Camnago, close to the Lake of Como, to fend off a widespread prejudice which implied that these tubers were poisonous. He debunked this myth by creating a wonderful yet unusual recipe that has now become one of Italy's most popular dishes. Gnocchi are appreciated all over the world and can be seasoned with whatever sauce you like, from classic tomato sauce to pesto and bolognese. What else can we say? Buon appetito!

Raspberry Caves

Sweden
by Linda Eriksson

PREPARATION TIME
10 minutes
COOKING TIME
15 minutes

1 Place cupcake cases on a tray and heat the oven to Gas Mark 6/200°C/400°F. Warm butter to room temperature and mix in a bowl with the sugar and vanilla flavouring.

2 Combine baking powder and flour, and mix into the butter-sugar a little at a time until the dough is easy to shape and roll. If the dough is dry or crumbles it means there is too much flour, so add a little milk until it is workable.

3 Divide the dough and roll to small balls about the size of walnuts, and place them in the paper cases. Use a finger or something small and round to push into the dough to make a small dip in the middle, then put a dollop of raspberry jam in the hole.

4 Bake in the oven for 12 – 15 minutes. Leave biscuits to cool under a tea towel and then store in a bag or tin.

Makes 30 biscuits

200g butter
100g sugar
1.5 tsp vanilla flavouring
1 tsp baking powder
300g plain flour
milk
raspberry jam

This recipe is special to me because it is a classic Swedish sweet biscuit which I grew up with, and it was always my favourite biscuit. Since I moved to the UK I have made and brought these biscuits to English tea parties and they were so popular that several people immediately wanted the recipe. After living here for years it means a lot to me when I can still make people excited by sharing something from my own culture, something that they haven't tried before. Of all the things I've shared with people from all corners of the world, my Swedish baking was always the most appreciated.

Memory by Linda Eriksson

Tinginys
The Lazy One

Lithuania
by Rita Hussain

PREPARATION TIME
10 minutes
COOKING TIME
4 hours

1 Crush the biscuits into small pieces.

2 Melt condensed milk, butter, dark and milk chocolate together in a pot on a low heat and mix it well. Take chocolate mix off the heat and add the crushed biscuits.

3 Roll mixture into desired shape and wrap it with cling film. Keep it in the fridge until it solidifies.

Serves 8-10

300-400g plain biscuits
1 can condensed milk
80g butter
100g dark chocolate
50g milk chocolate

There are hundreds of different versions of it but this is how my mom makes it. My whole family has a sweet tooth, my mom especially, so she got me used to eating sweets after any meal. This cake is something we would all eat together, but I always remember secretly sneaking back into the kitchen for more!

Memory by Rita Hussain, UCL

Draniki
Potato Pancakes

Belarus
by Anna Vasilyeva

PREPARATION TIME
10 minutes
COOKING TIME
5 minutes

1 Wash, peel, and grate the potatoes into a bowl. Add two eggs, a pinch of salt, and flour and mix.

2 Heat the olive oil in a frying pan, and use approximately two tablespoons of the mixture to create each pancake.

3 Fry the pancakes for 1-2 minutes, then flip them, frying for the same amount of time until golden. Serve with sour cream and butter or salted salmon (which is delicious too and very Russian/Belarusian).

Makes 12

5 potatoes
2 eggs
3 tbsp plain flour
pinch of salt
1 tbsp olive oil

This is still one of my all-time favourite dishes and they remind me of home like nothing else. As my whole family is originally from Belarus, my parents used to send me to live with my granny in her house in a tiny Belarusian village for the whole summer when I was a child. Each year she greeted me with these very simple but delicious potato pancakes. Now my mom cooks them for me when I visit my family in Russia.

Memory by Anna Vasilyeva, UCL

Spinach with Rice

Bulgaria
by Ivana Dimitrova

PREPARATION TIME
5 minutes
COOKING TIME
25 minutes

1 Wash all the ingredients. Heat oil and 30ml water in a pan over a low heat and add the chopped onions, frying until soft and translucent. Meanwhile, cut the spinach into strips and add to the pan. Then add the paprika and salt to taste. Cook for 5 minutes until spinach is soft, and add the tomatoes.

2 Add remaining water and rice to the pan, stirring from time to time to keep the bottom from burning. When the rice is cooked, turn off the hob and add the mixed herbs. Stir one more time, cover it and let it sit for about 10 minutes.

Serves 3-5

90ml olive oil
330ml water
600g spinach
2 large onions
200g rice
3 tomatoes, chopped
1 tsp paprika
1 tsp salt
1 tsp mixed herbs

SERVE WITH A SPOONFUL OF GREEK STYLE YOGURT ON TOP AND SOME BLACK PEPPER.

Second term of first year I just needed food that was different from pasta and pizza! My mom came to the rescue with this lovely recipe and saved the day as always. Perfect for busy (lazy) students, and for when you want to impress a guy/girl with some cooking skills, but you don't really have any. It is also nutritious and delicious, much healthier than pasta; with even greater health potential if you switch the white rice with brown.

Memory by Ivana Dimitrova, UCL.

AFRICA

Moroccan Chicken with Zesty Couscous

Morocco
by Kaysen Harlow

PREPARATION TIME
5 minutes
COOKING TIME
25 minutes

Serves 4

150g couscous
1 lemon, zest and juice
salt and pepper
1 tbsp olive oil
1 tbsp clear honey
4 skinless, boneless
   chicken breasts,
   sliced into large strips
2 tbsp ground cinnamon
2 tbsp ground cumin
2 tbsp ground ginger
4 chopped tomatoes
150ml chicken stock
1 red pepper chopped
150g fine green beans,
   trimmed
pomegranate seeds &
   coriander (optional)

1 Put the couscous, half the lemon zest, half the lemon juice, and 400ml water in a pot and cook over a medium heat.

2 Heat oil in a large non-stick frying pan, drizzle honey, cumin, ginger, cinnamon, salt and pepper over the chicken and cook over a medium heat for 5-6 minutes, until golden.

3 Mix in the tomatoes, stock, beans and remaining lemon zest and juice. Bring to the boil and simmer uncovered for 8-10 minutes or until the beans are tender.

4 Fork through the couscous to fluff it up, then serve with the chicken. Add pomegranate seeds and coriander (optional).

A holiday spent travelling throughout Morocco; the colours, the warmth, the culture and spices are fond memories I hold onto and reminisce about quite often. Whilst most Moroccan dishes are slow cooked in a tagine, this is my take on a simple and 30minute Moroccan dish sans tagine.

Memory by Kaysen Harlow, Cass Business School

Poitjie
A Pot of Stew

South Africa
by Nicholas Trataris

PREPARATION TIME
15 minutes
COOKING TIME
4 hours

Serves 8-12

4 large leeks, chopped
2 white onions, diced
2 red onions, diced
5 large carrots,
     chopped
6 tomatoes, chopped
1 whole bulb of garlic,
     crushed
2 red peppers, diced
2 yellow peppers, diced
1/4 bunch of coriander
1/4 bunch of parsley
1/4 bunch of thyme (1/8
     to season the meat)
1/4 bunch of rosemary
     (1/8 to season the
     meat)
750g smoked back
     bacon
2kg shin beef, cubed
     into 4cm pieces
750ml beer
500ml beef stock
5 bananas
3 tbsp vegetable oil

1 Season the shin beef in salt, pepper, rosemary, and thyme and seal in a hot pan with the oil.

2 Place all the chopped vegetables and herbs in a casserole dish with a touch of oil. Brown the vegetables slightly before adding the bananas.

3 Then add the bacon and the beef to the vegetables and after 15 minutes pour in the beef stock and beer.

4 Cook on an open fire or oven at Gas Mark 4/180°C/350°F for between 3-4 hours, stirring occasionally. Add more beer as and when required to maintain a thick liquid consistency.

The recipe is for a traditional South African dish called Poitjie (poy-key), normally cooked in a large cast iron pot known as a Poitjie pot. Being from South Africa, this is something that I grew up eating every weekend. To me it meant family and friends all together in one place sharing stories, jokes, and news with one another over some good food. As it is a very traditional dish it has become 'fine-tuned' by many South Africans, leading to many different variations and combinations.

Memory by Nicholas Trataris, University of East Anglia

ASIA

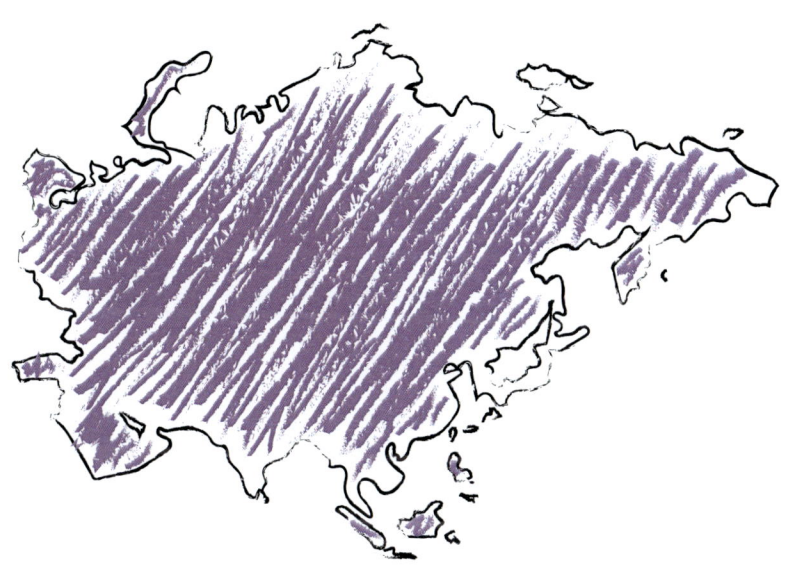

Juweri Gurtik
Soup and Dumplings

Karakalpak
by Gozzal Utemuratova

PREPARATION TIME
30 minutes
COOKING TIME
1 hour 10 minutes

Serves 4-5

DUMPLINGS
1kg corn flour
300g wheat flour
1 tsp salt
water

DRESSING
2 onions, sliced
soup

SOUP
1kg beef or turkey
3 onions, sliced
2 sweet peppers
3-4 carrots
3-4 tomatoes
4-5 potatoes
salt

To make the dumplings:

1 Boil a large pot of water seasoned with salt. Mix the corn flour and salty hot boiled water together in a bowl. Add the wheat flower slowly, mixing continuously. When the dough is combined, leave it to cool.

2 Separate the dough into small pieces and make small coin-shaped rounds.

To prepare dressing:

1 Place sliced onions into a small pot and add some soup, then simmer over a low heat for 3 minutes.

To prepare the soup:

1 Pour water into a large pot, add the meat and bring to a boil. Add all other ingredients to the soup and simmer for around 90 minutes.

2 Remove the meat and vegetables from the soup, and keep warm. Add dough coins into the soup and boil it for 20 minutes.

3 Remove cooked dumplings from the soup and arrange into a large plate. Place the meat and sliced vegetables on top of the dumplings, and add the dressing to serve. Portion out the soup into separate bowls and leave your guests to tuck in to the meat and dumplings.

This dish is special for me as I can eat this meal when my family gathers together at home. It reminds me of my childhood and my grandmother as she loved to treat us to this meal. I would help with the dumplings as it can take a long time, and she would tell me interesting stories of her life. Whenever I visit my home and have this meal I remember those sweet memories.

Memory by Gozzal Utemuratova, UCL

Pakora
Onion Bhajis

Pakistan
by Bilal Awan

PREPARATION TIME
10 minutes
COOKING TIME
15 minutes

1 Peel and chop the potatoes and onions. In a bowl, mix all the other ingredients, adding some water to make it into a paste-like consistency.

2 Add the onions, potatoes, and coriander and mix well.

3 Heat the oil for frying, and when hot drop a spoonful of the mixture into the oil, frying them until golden brown. Move bhajis around in the oil frequently.

Serves 4-6

2-3 potatoes
1 tsp baking powder
salt, to taste
225g gram flour
2 onions
½ tsp chilli powder
½ tsp cumin seeds
chopped coriander
    leaves
vegetable oil for frying

My mum would only ever make onion bhajis on special occasions. If guests were coming over or it was a special day, I knew when I heard them frying in the kitchen that something was going on that day. I remember trying to sneak and steal a couple while she was still cooking them, because they're always best when they're hot and fresh. Naturally she tried to stop me, but I was always just quick enough to get at least a few before she hit me with the ladle she was using to fish them out of the oil!

Memory by Bilal Awan, UCL

Lamb Stew with Carrots

China
by Yunrui Ge

PREPARATION TIME
10 minutes
COOKING TIME
43 minutes

1 Dice the lamb chops and boil in water for 8 minutes. Heat the oil in a pan and stir-fry the ginger and garlic slices until softened. Add the boiled lamb to the pan and fry for 5minutes.

2 Boil some water in a large pot and add the cooked lamb. Peel and dice the carrots and add to the pot. Season with salt, soybean sauce, orange peel, and simmer for 30 minutes.

3 Slice the spring onions into approximately 4cm-long pieces and add to the pot. Boil for 10 minutes while adding sugar or other seasonings to your taste. Serve in a bowl, and optionally with rice.

Serves 2-3

4 lamb chops
2 tbsp oil
2 carrots
3 spring onion bunches
ginger, sliced
garlic cloves, sliced
orange peel
salt, sugar, and soybean
    sauce to taste

In my hometown, every household
will have this lamb stew when winter
comes. It is believed that eating lamb
in winter will keep the body warm from
the inside. It's just the taste of home!

Memory by Yunrui Ge, UCL

Filipino Chicken Adobo

The Philippines
by Karina Maduro

PREPARATION TIME
5 minutes
COOKING TIME
45 minutes

1 Combine chicken, soy sauce and garlic into a large pot, adding water, vinegar, salt and pepper.

2 Simmer for 20-30 minutes on a medium heat until chicken is tender. When half of the sauce is reduced, remove the sauce and place in a separate pot. Add cooking oil and sauté ingredients. Add sauce back into pot and mix.

3 Serve with rice for authentic Filipino experience.

Serves 5

1kg chicken
1 tsp salt
½ tsp pepper
30ml vinegar
55ml water
30ml soy sauce

When I was at university for my undergrad, my cooking skills mostly consisted of boiling pasta and adding Dolmio sauce. So I loved coming back to my mum's home cooking and her classic Filipino recipes, particularly her chicken adobo.

Memory by Karina Maduro, UCL

Mom's Carrot Cake

Abu Dhabi, United Arab Emirates
by Mahnoor Mahmood

PREPARATION TIME
15 minutes
COOKING TIME
30 minutes

1 Preheat oven to Gas Mark 4/180°C/350°F.

2 Combine flour, bicarbonate of soda, baking powder, ground cinnamon, and salt in a bowl.

3 In a separate bowl beat the eggs, and whisk in the brown sugar. Add egg mixture to the dry ingredients along with the vegetable oil and mix well. The batter will be thick. Fold the carrots and walnuts into the batter.

4 Pour mixture into a 9x5 bread tin or an 8 square inch baking pan and bake for approximately 25-30 minutes or until a toothpick inserted in the center comes out clean. Leave to cool and cut into slices.

Serves 8-10

150g flour
1 tsp bicarbonate of
    soda
1 tsp baking powder
1 tsp ground cinnamon
1/2 tsp salt
100g vegetable oil
175g light brown sugar
2 eggs
150-225g grated carrot
75g chopped walnuts
    (optional)

CONTRIBUTORS

This cookbook would not have been possible without the generous support of the following people. Thank you so much for everything, and happy eating!

Heather Everill
Sarfaraz Awan
Joyce Watson
Christian Ashton
Rebecca Atkinson
Catriona Beamish
Zlata Burova
Sharon Carr
Meg and Clarke Conant
Tessa Conradie
Kate Griffiths
Iftee Hussain
Jim King
Mike and Mary Jo King
Mike and Diane King
Bill and Lois LaBarge
Mohit Sachdeva

Cristhopper Armenta
Charlotte Parker
Mary Beth Powell
Melanie G Robinson
Kimberly Swayze
Sumit Tickoo
Anuj Tyagi
Rich Wills
Patricio Escobar
Sandra Munoz
Luz Rubio
Matt King
Karen LaBarge-King
Ehchiragh

INDEX BY COUNTRY

INDEX BY INGREDIENT

CONVERSIONS

Oven Temperatures

Gas Mark	°F	°C
1	275°	140°
2	300°	150°
3	325°	170°
4	350°	180°
5	375°	190°
6	400°	200°
7	425°	220°
8	450°	230°
9	475°	240°

Volume

Imperial	Metric
2 fl oz	55 ml
3 fl oz	75 ml
5 fl oz ($^1/_4$)	150 ml
10 fl oz ($^1/_2$)	275 ml
1 pint	570 ml
1 $^1/_4$ pint	725 ml
1 $^3/_4$ pint	1 litre
2 pint	1.2 litre
2 $^1/_2$ pint	1.5 litre
4 pint	2.25 litre

Liquid Conversions

American	Imperial	Metric
1 teaspoon	1 teaspoon	5 ml
$^1/_2$ fl oz	1 tablespoon	15 ml
$^1/_4$ cup	4 tablespoons	55 ml
$^1/_2$ cup plus 2 tablespoons	$^1/_4$ pint	150 ml
1 $^1/_4$ cups	$^1/_2$ pint	275 ml
1 pint / 16 fl oz	$^3/_4$ pint	450 ml
2 $^1/_2$ pint / 5 cups	2 pints	1.2 litres
10 pint	8 pints	4.8 litres

American Cup Conversions

American	Imperial	Metric
1 cup flour	5 oz	150 g
1 cup caster and granulated sugar	8 oz	225 g
1 cup brown sugar	6 oz	175 g
1 cup butter / margarine / lard	8 oz	225 g
1 cup sultanas / raisins	7 oz	200 g
1 cup currants	5 oz	150 g
1 cup ground almonds	4 oz	110 g
1 cup golden syrup	12 oz	350 g
1 cup uncooked rice	7 oz	200 g
1 cup grated cheese	4 oz	110 g
1 stick butter	4 oz	110 g

Dimensions

Imperial	Metric
$1/2$ inch	3 mm
$1/4$ inch	5 mm
$1/2$ inch	1 cm
$3/4$ inch	2 cm
1 inch	2.5 cm
1 $1/4$ inch	3 cm
1 $1/2$ inch	4 cm
1 $3/4$ inch	4.5 cm
2 inch	5 cm
2 $1/2$ inch	6 cm
3 inch	7.5 cm
3 $1/2$ inch	9 cm
4 inch	10 cm
5 inch	13 cm
5 $1/4$ inch	13.5 cm
6 inch	15 cm
6 $1/2$ inch	16 cm
7 inch	18 cm
7 $1/2$ inch	19 cm
8 inch	20 cm
9 inch	23 cm
9 $1/2$ inch	24 cm
10 inch	25.5 cm
11 inch	28 cm
12 inch	30 cm

Weights

Imperial	Metric
$1/2$ oz	10 g
$3/4$ oz	20 g
1 oz	25 g
1 $1/2$ oz	40 g
2 oz	50 g
2 $1/2$ oz	60 g
3 oz	75 g
4 oz	110 g
4 $1/2$ oz	125 g
5 oz	150 g
6 oz	175 g
7 oz	200 g
8 oz	225 g
9 oz	250 g
10 oz	275 g
12 oz	350 g
1 lb	450 g
1 lb 8 oz	700 g
2 lb	900 g
3 lb	1.35 kg